By Me, About Me

By Me, About Me

WRITING YOUR LIFE

Victoria Ryce

RAINCOAST BOOKS

Vancouver

*This book is dedicated to everyone who has shared a life story
with me, especially my sweetheart, Michael*

First published in 1997 by

Raincoast Books
8680 Cambie Street
Vancouver, B.C.
V6P 6M9
(604) 323-7100

1 3 5 7 9 10 8 6 4 2

CANADIAN CATALOGUING IN PUBLICATION DATA

Ryce, Victoria.
By me, about me

ISBN 1-55192-064-6

1. Autobiography – Authorship. I. Title.
CT25.R92 1997   808'.06692   C96-910699-8

Designed by Dean Allen
Edited by Rachelle Kanefsky

Printed and bound in Canada

Contents

How to Get Started

By Me, About Me is a book with the most interesting main character in the world. It is a book about *you*. Here, right in this book, is a place for you to record your life stories. This is where you can recall people, events, ideas, and dreams that matter to you.

Most of us would be secretly thrilled to have our life stories written, yet we shy away from the attention. We see men and women being interviewed on television or in magazines, but somehow we don't think that we, too, have interesting stories to tell and valuable ideas to share.

On the contrary. Each of us has unique stories to tell. When I realized this, I thought, Why can't everyone write their life stories? So I began one night by taking a book of blank pages and, on the first page, I listed the reasons why I was writing down the stories of my life. That was the easy part. Then I couldn't decide what to include or where to start. So I began to ask questions to prompt myself. In other words, I interviewed myself, as if I were a famous person. I asked questions about where I grew up, what I remembered most, and what was important to me. For example, here's one piece from my thoughts on books:

> I love reading. It is a gift my mother gave to me. What I have come to understand about the many books I've read is that they were like friends to me. I could read the books and feel as though I were on the same wavelength as the people who wrote them.

At first it seemed silly, talking to myself, but after a while my thoughts really began to flow. When I finally finished writing two months later, I found that I had filled the whole book fairly easily. I also realized how wonderful it would be if my husband, family, and friends had a way to record their own thoughts. That's when the idea for *By Me, About Me* was born.

Perhaps you have thought of writing down some of the things that have happened to you but the time or place wasn't exactly right. Or you may have thought you didn't have anything to say, or felt that you couldn't put it in writing. One man who had some of these feelings told me about a teacher he had: "She had knuckles the size of quarters turned on their side from arthritis. Even though she was a short little thing, when she rapped you with one of those knuckles, you knew it." I love that story. It is as unique and special to him as your stories are to you.

Everyone I have ever met has an interesting life story to tell. A woman once told me all three of her daughters were pregnant at the same time. What a story of coincidences! And a few years ago I met the fellow who suggested the original idea for salt-and-vinegar potato chips. All of these stories are priceless, and so are yours. They deserve to be recorded.

To give shape to your stories, *By Me, About Me* is arranged in sections with titles such as "Childhood and Family Adventures" and "Views of the World." Within each section there are many thought-provoking prompts – like "The most bizarre thing to happen in my childhood" and "What money means to me" – followed by a page or two for you to fill in with your stories. You can write as much or as little as you like on each page. At the end of each section you'll also find some miniature memory prompts to fill in that will add to the portrait of your life. This is where, for example, you can include the name of your oldest friend and the sports, games, or instruments you played in childhood.

Reading the prompts and writing your stories will most certainly release more of your memories. The prompts will give you a starting point to begin your writing. However, if you find a certain topic doesn't suit you, take out the words that don't reflect your life and write in those words that do. Of course, you will probably have certain stories that hold special significance for you alone. These can be jotted down on the blank pages provided at the back of the book in the section entitled "Other Thoughts."

You may find that as you write your stories you'll discover some things you didn't know when you started. Sometimes by writing things down we can examine them anew. Often we have thoughts running through our heads that only begin to make sense when they form some sort of order. While writing my book, and later, when rereading it, I thought more about past events. Here's one piece that I wrote:

> My father told me that one Christmas, when he was a boy, all he got as a present was an orange. Perhaps that's why every year my brother and I got apples and oranges in our stockings. Perhaps it was a carryover or reminder to appreciate the good times. Not for us, but for him.

When I was writing my stories, I often did little sketches to help get my feelings on the page. I also included pictures in my book, glued in little sayings, and put in cards and photographs that had meaning for me. There are no set rules for writing your life stories, which means you can create your book to be anything you wish. In fact, you may want to give this book your own title. A friend of mine said he was going to give his copy of *By Me, About Me* the title "Wild Thing."

By Me, About Me is not meant to be a journal or a diary, which serve a different purpose. I've written journals for about 20 years, and while I find them interesting to reread, I'm not quite sure why I wrote some of the things I did. These journals contain items that I felt were important at the time, such as daily events. However, the thoughts expressed are a bit scattered and they don't fully reflect who I am. Also, many people never record happy events in their journals. Instead they tend to use them as dumping grounds for writing about their bad days.

This book is also not intended to be a psychological study of yourself. I have read many of these kinds of "know yourself" books and have always felt a certain dissatisfaction with them. I think it is because these books are often about other people's stories and I have always felt a need for a book about me. After I wrote my own book of stories, I felt I knew more about myself. Things came to light and some things suddenly made sense. I also felt happy, which is what I hope writing your stories will make you feel, too.

This book can be a record of things that have influenced you. It can be a record of your opinions. It will give you a chance to put down what you know and, perhaps, through the prompts at the top of each page, discover what you have yet to know.

Everyone has a story to tell because all of our families and friends are famous to us. I use the term family here in the broadest sense. Family is meant to include whoever you wish – a nuclear family, an extended family, or a family of friends. Whatever the case may be, having your family stories on record means they can be enjoyed over and over again.

What was she like? What was he like? What was it like when you were growing up? If you have ever been asked these questions and racked your brain for information, *By Me, About Me* will help jog your memory. Ten years from now I think you'll find it a pleasurable experience to sit down with someone for an afternoon and read portions of your book to them.

Both where we live and our living arrangements have changed dramatically over the years. No longer do friends and relatives live in the same village or even in the same country. This means many stories that were once told around the dinner table or at family gatherings are now lost. This book is a place where you can recapture that rich history.

And in the past, when the means of communication were not as instant as they are today, people wrote more letters to one another. Through such letters we have learned a lot about the day-to-day activities, thoughts, and feelings of our ancestors, the personal side of history. Today, with the telephone so handy and when the camera or camcorder gets the picture, people don't write as many letters. Unfortunately words get lost in the air and pictures only tell one side of the story.

I believe these technological conveniences do not give the same feeling as the written word. Our choice of words says something about us. The color of ink in our pen may also say something about who we are. The slant of our handwriting is our own. One of my friends sends each of her letters with a little drawing on the front of the envelope. That makes them uniquely hers. When you write your book, it will have many elements that are uniquely you, things you may not even recognize until you put them down on paper.

By Me, About Me asks only that you be yourself. There are no deadlines to meet. Write in this book at your convenience or when you feel inspired. Fill in those pages that you choose to and leave the others blank. Open your book to any page and start there if you like. The start and finish points are up to you. Add information later if you wish, or cross some things out. If you find you are having difficulty getting started, imagine that you are being interviewed and telling someone about yourself.

You can start writing today. Write in the quiet of your room or in the noise of a restaurant. Write this book as a joint life story with a friend or relative. At a special occasion, have everyone who is there write one page. Write it for yourself, for your eyes only, or write it for another. Write it for someone who isn't even born yet. Write it for a person who will appreciate it years from now. Write *By Me, About Me* for your own reasons.

Whatever you decide, now is the time for you to delve into this exciting new book – your own bestseller, all about the famous, one and only *you*. *By Me, About Me* is for everyone, because everyone has great life stories to tell. Some are sad, some are happy, and some are incredibly funny. But they all share one quality: they are all unique. I hope you enjoy bringing your stories to the page.

Childhood and Family Adventures

While your childhood may seem as if it happened a long time ago, you probably have many distinct memories of it. Writing down these memories will trigger even more of them.

As a child, the world seems defined by a limited space. For the most part, there is your home, your friends' homes, your school, and where you played. When my husband and I went back to the street where he grew up, he laughed and said, "I remember it being much bigger. I wasn't allowed to ride my bike to the fire station because it was too far away and I might get lost. Now I see it's just at the corner."

How you see the world as a child is also very fresh. You discover things for the first time. Daily events, like going to school, hold great importance. You measure how tall you are growing. You say your age with such precision: "Yes, I am six and a half." And adults always try to make you go to bed too early, or just when something exciting is about to happen.

Many of our first impressions stay with us for life. Here is a place for you to think back and write about some of your early experiences, those that shaped you into the person you are today.

My name, or names, and how I came to be called that

_____

_____

_____

_____

_____

_____

_____

_____

_____

_____

_____

_____

_____

_____

_____

_____

_____

_____

My parents' names and a bit about them

_____

_____

_____

_____

_____

_____

_____

_____

_____

_____

_____

_____

_____

_____

_____

_____

_____

Where and when I was born

_____

_____

_____

_____

_____

_____

_____

_____

_____

_____

_____

_____

_____

_____

_____

_____

_____

_____

My very first memory

_____

_____

_____

_____

_____

_____

_____

_____

_____

_____

_____

_____

_____

_____

_____

_____

_____

_____

My very first memory . . . *continued*

_____

_____

_____

_____

_____

_____

_____

_____

_____

_____

_____

_____

_____

_____

_____

_____

_____

Family members I grew up with

_____

_____

_____

_____

_____

_____

_____

_____

_____

_____

_____

_____

_____

_____

_____

_____

_____

Family members I grew up with . . . *continued*

_____

_____

_____

_____

_____

_____

_____

_____

_____

_____

_____

_____

_____

_____

_____

_____

_____

_____

Stories I was told by my family

_____

_____

_____

_____

_____

_____

_____

_____

_____

_____

_____

_____

_____

_____

_____

_____

_____

_____

Stories I was told by my family . . .*continued*

_____

_____

_____

_____

_____

_____

_____

_____

_____

_____

_____

_____

_____

_____

_____

_____

_____

_____

The schools I went to – names, addresses, impressions

_____

_____

_____

_____

_____

_____

_____

_____

_____

_____

_____

_____

_____

_____

_____

_____

_____

_____

_____

_____

Teachers I remember

_____

_____

_____

_____

_____

_____

_____

_____

_____

_____

_____

_____

_____

_____

_____

_____

_____

_____

Toys I played with

_____

_____

_____

_____

_____

_____

_____

Pets that I had

_____

_____

_____

_____

_____

_____

_____

_____

Where we lived and what it was like

_____

_____

_____

_____

_____

_____

_____

_____

_____

_____

_____

_____

_____

_____

_____

_____

_____

_____

The most bizarre thing to happen in my childhood

_____

_____

_____

_____

_____

_____

_____

Smells I remember

_____

_____

_____

_____

_____

_____

_____

My experiences with doctors and medicine

_____

_____

_____

_____

_____

_____

_____

_____

_____

_____

_____

_____

_____

_____

_____

_____

_____

Family trips

_____

_____

_____

_____

_____

_____

_____

_____

_____

_____

_____

_____

_____

_____

_____

_____

_____

_____

What I wanted to be when I grew up

_____

_____

_____

_____

_____

_____

_____

_____

_____

_____

_____

_____

_____

_____

_____

I amused myself by _____

_____

_____

_____

I loved to eat _____

_____

_____

_____

My best friend was _____

_____

_____

_____

The funniest thing I remember was _____

_____

_____

_____

What really scared me was _____

_____

_____

_____

My favorite piece of clothing was_____

_____

_____

_____

_____

Sports and games I played were _____

_____

_____

_____

_____

Music I liked was_____

_____

_____

_____

_____

My favorite book was _____

_____

_____

_____

_____

Being an Adolescent

Being a teenager is so much different than being a child. You know so much more. In fact, at times you feel as if you know it all. For some people the teenage years are their best years, while for others they are the worst. It is when the growth of mind, body, and hormones completely takes over. It is a time of conflict when conforming or rebelling seem to be the only two choices. You are a grab bag of emotions, and your confidence level rises and falls depending on what happens in your day.

How you look, what you wear, who your friends are, and what you do, all of these external things take on more meaning. As a fashion victim, I recall wearing laced brown suede platform shoes that a boy named Bob referred to as gladiator boots. One moment I thought I was so cool and then an instant later I thought I would die.

In this section you have a chance to relive some of your youth by recording the events and feelings that were important, embarrassing, life-changing, sad, emotional, or hilarious. What happened in your search for adulthood will likely include things you both want to forget forever and things you want to remember again and again. Ah, yes, the good old days.

What my teenage life was like

_____

_____

_____

_____

_____

_____

_____

_____

_____

_____

_____

_____

_____

_____

_____

_____

_____

_____

My teenage idols

_____

_____

_____

_____

_____

_____

_____

_____

_____

_____

_____

_____

_____

_____

_____

_____

_____

_____

_____

_____

Schools I went to

_____

_____

_____

_____

_____

_____

_____

_____

_____

_____

_____

_____

_____

_____

_____

_____

_____

_____

_____

Subjects I remember the most

_____

_____

_____

_____

_____

_____

_____

_____

_____

_____

_____

_____

_____

_____

_____

_____

_____

_____

Teachers who influenced me

_____

_____

_____

_____

_____

_____

_____

_____

_____

_____

_____

_____

_____

_____

_____

_____

_____

_____

The most significant thing that happened to me

_____

_____

_____

_____

_____

_____

_____

_____

_____

_____

_____

_____

_____

_____

_____

_____

_____

Who my pals were

_____

_____

_____

_____

_____

_____

_____

_____

_____

_____

_____

_____

_____

_____

_____

The first person I fell in love with

_____

_____

_____

_____

_____

_____

_____

_____

_____

_____

_____

_____

_____

_____

_____

_____

_____

_____

_____

_____

Competitions I participated in

_____

_____

_____

_____

_____

_____

_____

_____

_____

_____

_____

_____

_____

_____

_____

_____

_____

What I liked to do most

_____

_____

_____

_____

_____

_____

_____

_____

_____

_____

_____

_____

_____

_____

_____

_____

Getting caught doing what I knew was not allowed

What learning to drive was like for me

_____

_____

_____

_____

_____

_____

_____

_____

_____

_____

_____

_____

_____

_____

_____

Summer jobs I had

_____

_____

_____

_____

_____

_____

_____

_____

_____

_____

_____

_____

_____

_____

_____

_____

The funniest thing I ever did with someone from my family

_____

_____

_____

_____

_____

_____

_____

_____

_____

_____

_____

_____

_____

_____

_____

_____

_____

_____

A turning point in my youth

_____

_____

_____

_____

_____

_____

_____

_____

_____

_____

_____

_____

_____

_____

_____

_____

_____

What I looked like

_____

_____

_____

_____

_____

_____

_____

_____

_____

_____

_____

_____

_____

_____

_____

_____

_____

The music I listened to was _____

_____

_____

_____

_____

Movies I went to see were _____

_____

_____

_____

_____

The places I hung out were _____

_____

_____

_____

_____

The clothes I most liked to wear were _____

_____

_____

_____

_____

_____

I have a scar on my _____

and I got it _____

_____

_____

_____

_____

Sports, games, or instruments I played were _____

_____

_____

_____

_____

_____

The thing I thought was the most fabulous thing on earth was _____

_____

_____

_____

_____

_____

_____

Life as an Adult

While 21 is the age you officially enter adulthood, some people feel they are adults long before then and others realize they're not a kid anymore years later. In part, moving beyond adolescence has to do with the milestones you pass. You may move away from home, start working, get married, have children, travel, pay taxes, or all of these. Often, whenever you do something that you associate with your parents, you feel as if you've reached a milestone. For example, putting money away for my retirement jolted me into thinking I was an adult and that I could no longer use my student card, an illusion I had carried for quite some time.

Becoming an adult means different things to different people. Some look forward to adulthood, others try to push it away. It includes responsibility, and not everyone is ready to take that on. As my friend Jean says, "In youth nobody expects anything of you." Adulthood means having to stand on your own two feet. It means taking care of yourself, and for many, it means taking care of others, too.

When you grow up, you have increased responsibilities and obligations, but you also have more freedom and you are able to make decisions for yourself. Your own taste and your own style show up in how you dress, what your home looks like, and what you choose to eat. Yes, the person shaping your future – the adult person in charge – is you.

When you think about it now, you may be stunned at a few of the decisions you've made over your adult life: some positive, some negative, and some surprising. Ultimately, though, adulthood is about getting smarter, understanding more, and inevitably, it is an ongoing process as your life unfolds.

Moving away from home

_____

_____

_____

_____

_____

_____

_____

_____

_____

_____

_____

_____

_____

_____

_____

_____

_____

My first real job

_____

_____

_____

_____

_____

_____

_____

_____

_____

_____

_____

_____

_____

_____

_____

_____

_____

_____

The best boss I ever had and the worst one

_____

_____

_____

_____

_____

_____

_____

_____

_____

_____

_____

_____

_____

_____

_____

_____

_____

How I am different from or similar to my parents

_____

_____

_____

_____

_____

_____

_____

_____

_____

_____

_____

_____

_____

_____

_____

_____

_____

_____

How I am different from or similar to my parents . . .*continued*

_____

_____

_____

_____

_____

_____

_____

_____

_____

_____

_____

_____

_____

_____

_____

_____

_____

_____

What I thank my parents for

_____

_____

_____

_____

_____

_____

_____

_____

_____

_____

_____

_____

_____

_____

_____

Things I have done to change the way I look

_____

_____

_____

_____

_____

_____

_____

_____

_____

_____

_____

_____

_____

_____

_____

_____

_____

_____

Love and maybe marriage

_____

_____

_____

_____

_____

_____

_____

_____

_____

_____

_____

_____

_____

_____

_____

_____

_____

_____

_____

_____

_____

Love and maybe marriage . . . *continued*

_____

_____

_____

_____

_____

_____

_____

_____

_____

_____

_____

_____

_____

_____

_____

_____

_____

_____

Births

_____

_____

_____

_____

_____

_____

_____

_____

_____

_____

_____

_____

_____

_____

_____

_____

_____

_____

Deaths

_____

_____

_____

_____

_____

_____

_____

_____

_____

_____

_____

_____

_____

_____

_____

_____

_____

_____

_____

_____

_____

Where my career has taken me

The major accomplishment of my life so far

_____

_____

_____

_____

_____

_____

_____

_____

_____

_____

_____

_____

_____

_____

_____

_____

_____

_____

A dream I had that I realized

_____

_____

_____

_____

_____

_____

_____

_____

_____

_____

_____

_____

_____

_____

_____

_____

_____

_____

Risks I have taken

Where I live now and how I feel about my home

_____

_____

_____

_____

_____

_____

_____

_____

_____

_____

_____

_____

_____

_____

_____

_____

_____

_____

Someone I have not spoken to in years

_____

_____

_____

_____

_____

_____

_____

_____

_____

_____

_____

_____

_____

_____

_____

_____

_____

What I have built or made

_____

_____

_____

_____

_____

_____

_____

_____

_____

_____

_____

_____

_____

_____

_____

_____

_____

_____

Where I have traveled

Where I have traveled . . .*continued*

_____

_____

_____

_____

_____

_____

_____

_____

_____

_____

_____

_____

_____

_____

_____

_____

_____

_____

Why I consider myself traditional, modern, or unconventional

_____

_____

_____

_____

_____

_____

_____

_____

_____

_____

_____

_____

_____

_____

_____

_____

_____

_____

Things that really strike my funny bone

_____

_____

_____

_____

_____

_____

_____

_____

_____

_____

_____

_____

_____

_____

_____

_____

What has really changed from childhood to adulthood is _____

_____

_____

_____

Colors I like to have around me are _____

_____

_____

_____

My all-time favorite movie is _____

_____

_____

_____

What I like to drink is _____

_____

_____

_____

When I'm sick, this food makes me feel better: _____

_____

_____

_____

_____

My strengths are _____

_____

_____

_____

_____

_____

I wish I could stop _____

_____

_____

_____

_____

My oldest friend is _____

_____

_____

_____

_____

In my free time I like to _____

_____

_____

_____

_____

Views of the World

Each of us sees the world in a unique way. This is what makes people so interesting. At a party just introduce a seemingly harmless topic, such as food or travel, and you are bound to have 10 different reactions. Some of our views are formed through our home life, while others are influenced by our personal experiences, reading, or observations of events developing in the world. Thinking about your views of the world gives you a rare chance to reflect on some of the most important beliefs you hold, and how you came to hold those beliefs.

When I was working on this book, I had a black rotary-dial phone. Somehow all of the advanced telephone technology just missed me. People would plead with me to get a fax machine and special phone services so they could get in touch with me whenever they wanted. They told me to get into today's world of communications. I have resisted because it means less privacy to me. Where does this world-view come from? I'm still trying to figure it out.

Changes I have seen and how I would change the world

_____

_____

_____

_____

_____

_____

_____

_____

_____

_____

_____

_____

_____

_____

_____

_____

_____

_____

_____

Changes I have seen and how I would change the world . . .*continued*

_____

_____

_____

_____

_____

_____

_____

_____

_____

_____

_____

_____

_____

_____

_____

_____

_____

_____

The role spirituality has played in my life

My thoughts on superstition, fantasy, or magic

What I am tolerant and intolerant of

Reasons why I would, or would not, get involved with politics

_____

_____

_____

_____

_____

_____

_____

_____

_____

_____

_____

_____

_____

_____

_____

_____

_____

_____

_____

How I feel about the environment

_____

_____

_____

_____

_____

_____

_____

_____

_____

_____

_____

_____

_____

_____

_____

_____

_____

My thoughts on buildings and architecture

_____

_____

_____

_____

_____

_____

_____

_____

_____

_____

_____

_____

_____

_____

_____

_____

_____

_____

What money means to me

_____

_____

_____

_____

_____

_____

_____

_____

_____

_____

_____

_____

_____

_____

_____

_____

_____

_____

_____

_____

When I think about love, this is what I think about

_____

_____

_____

_____

_____

_____

_____

_____

_____

_____

_____

_____

_____

_____

_____

_____

_____

What independence means to me

_____

_____

_____

_____

_____

_____

_____

_____

_____

_____

_____

_____

_____

_____

_____

_____

_____

_____

This is how I feel about dancing

_____

_____

_____

_____

_____

_____

_____

What I would walk a mile to avoid

_____

_____

_____

_____

_____

_____

_____

_____

If I could pass on only one recipe, this would be it

_____

_____

_____

_____

_____

_____

_____

_____

_____

_____

_____

_____

_____

_____

_____

_____

_____

_____

_____

_____

What television means to me

_____

_____

_____

_____

_____

_____

_____

_____

_____

_____

_____

_____

_____

_____

_____

_____

_____

_____

My feelings about art and creativity

_____

_____

_____

_____

_____

_____

_____

_____

_____

_____

_____

_____

_____

_____

_____

_____

_____

_____

How I help other people

_____

_____

_____

_____

_____

_____

_____

_____

_____

_____

_____

_____

_____

_____

_____

_____

_____

_____

What I notice about technology

_____

_____

_____

_____

_____

_____

_____

_____

_____

_____

_____

_____

_____

_____

_____

_____

_____

_____

_____

_____

_____

Sayings that have meaning for me are _____

_____

_____

_____

I would take these three things on a deserted island with me: _____

_____

_____

_____

If I didn't live where I do, I'd like to live _____

_____

_____

_____

In my former life I was a _____

_____

_____

_____

What I love most about my country is _____

_____

_____

_____

_____

The Inner Self

People see the outside of you but only you know what is going on inside. Your thoughts, ideas, and dreams are known only to you and to those you tell. Some people are open to telling you a lot about themselves while others prefer to hold this kind of information back. Either way, revealing ourselves is a delicate process.

Your inner life is often your emotional life. It is where you keep your feelings of pride, joy, embarrassment, disappointment, sorrow, and hope. The inner you is where you store things that have had a life-changing effect on you. It is where you go to process information when you are making big decisions. It is where you maintain your self-image.

And sometimes what the world sees – the outer you – doesn't match up with what you're thinking. I once told my husband that sometimes I don't feel very confident. He told me no one would ever believe me because I went out into the world with such force. I realized I did this to create enough momentum so that I wouldn't be afraid. But only I knew that.

We all live with these kinds of contradictions, ideas, and impressions. They form our inner selves, a vital part of who we are. Here, in this section, you can explore some of the private thoughts and inner feelings that make you who you are.

The wildest thing I have ever done

_____

_____

_____

_____

_____

_____

_____

_____

_____

_____

_____

_____

_____

_____

_____

_____

_____

_____

My secrets

How I would describe myself

_____

_____

_____

_____

_____

_____

_____

_____

_____

_____

_____

_____

_____

_____

_____

_____

_____

_____

The saddest day of my life

What I feel proud of

_____

_____

_____

_____

_____

_____

_____

_____

_____

_____

_____

_____

_____

_____

_____

_____

_____

Answers I still don't have

_____

_____

_____

_____

_____

_____

_____

_____

_____

_____

_____

_____

_____

_____

_____

_____

_____

_____

What most people don't know about me

_____

_____

_____

_____

_____

_____

_____

_____

_____

_____

_____

_____

_____

_____

_____

_____

My ambitions

What overjoys me

The hardest lesson I have learned in life

How I feel about my body

_____

_____

_____

_____

_____

_____

_____

_____

_____

_____

_____

_____

_____

_____

_____

_____

_____

_____

What I feel about sex

_____

_____

_____

_____

_____

_____

_____

_____

_____

_____

_____

_____

_____

_____

_____

_____

_____

_____

The most romantic time I ever spent

_____

_____

_____

_____

_____

_____

_____

_____

_____

_____

_____

_____

_____

_____

_____

_____

The most romantic time I ever spent . . .*continued*

_____

_____

_____

_____

_____

_____

_____

_____

_____

_____

_____

_____

_____

_____

_____

_____

_____

_____

What inspires me

_____

_____

_____

_____

_____

_____

_____

_____

_____

_____

_____

_____

_____

_____

_____

_____

_____

_____

What I have yet to do with my life

Traumas I have overcome

_____

_____

_____

_____

_____

_____

_____

_____

_____

_____

_____

_____

_____

_____

_____

_____

_____

What retirement means to me

_____

_____

_____

_____

_____

_____

_____

_____

_____

_____

_____

_____

_____

_____

_____

_____

_____

My opinions that have changed over time

To feel secure I need_____

_____

_____

_____

Something I have always wanted to have is _____

_____

_____

_____

What I like most about myself is _____

_____

_____

_____

The person I most admire is _____

_____

_____

_____

What I hope people say about me is _____

_____

_____

_____

Imaginings

What if…? How could…? When might…? Your imagination is an incredible gift. It is the place where dreams and ideas begin. It is the place where you can start to see a different future.

Our imaginations are very powerful. At one point I had to imagine what this book would be like. By telling other people about the idea, I was able to get them to believe in it, too. And now you are holding in your hands something that once was just in my imagination.

Your imagination can take you many places. It can be serious or playful. Who hasn't thought about what would happen if they won a million dollars? Here is the place to write down what you would do. If you had three wishes, what would they be? Write them down. What will you be like 10 years from now? Where will you be living? You don't know either of these things for sure, but you can imagine. There are no right or wrong answers when you use your imagination. That is part of the thrill.

Dreaming and imagining are exciting and can even be therapeutic. So, in this section, let your thoughts run wild.

Things I would say if I was sitting alone with the head of my country

_____

_____

_____

_____

_____

_____

_____

_____

_____

_____

_____

_____

_____

_____

_____

_____

_____

_____

_____

_____

This is my ideal vacation

What will be written for my epitaph

_____

_____

_____

_____

_____

_____

_____

_____

_____

_____

_____

_____

_____

_____

_____

_____

If there were no limits on me, this is what I would do

_____

_____

_____

_____

_____

_____

_____

_____

_____

_____

_____

_____

_____

_____

_____

_____

_____

A letter I would write to a loved one

_____

_____

_____

_____

_____

_____

_____

_____

_____

_____

_____

_____

_____

_____

_____

_____

_____

_____

If I received a million dollars, this is what would happen

_____

_____

_____

_____

_____

_____

_____

_____

_____

_____

_____

_____

_____

_____

_____

_____

_____

_____

What I see when I picture myself 10 years from now

_____

_____

_____

_____

_____

_____

_____

_____

_____

_____

_____

_____

_____

_____

_____

_____

_____

_____

If I could be the star of a movie, this is the one I would choose

_____

_____

_____

_____

_____

_____

_____

_____

_____

_____

_____

_____

_____

_____

_____

_____

_____

My favorite room would look like this

_____

_____

_____

_____

_____

_____

_____

_____

_____

_____

_____

_____

_____

_____

_____

_____

_____

_____

_____

If I could change one thing about the way I look, this would be it

_____

_____

_____

_____

_____

_____

_____

_____

_____

_____

_____

_____

_____

_____

_____

_____

A time in history I would like to be transported to

_____

_____

_____

_____

_____

_____

_____

_____

_____

_____

_____

_____

_____

_____

_____

_____

_____

If I could be someone else for a day, this is who
I would be and this is what I would do

_____

_____

_____

_____

_____

_____

_____

_____

_____

_____

_____

_____

_____

_____

_____

_____

Three famous people (from the past or present)
I would like to invite to my dinner party

_____

_____

_____

_____

_____

_____

_____

_____

_____

_____

_____

_____

_____

_____

_____

_____

How the world will look in the year 2050

If I had three wishes, I would like a new_____, an old

_____, and a reconditioned _____

What I predict will happen one year from now is _____

_____

_____

_____

I would like to be reincarnated as _____

_____

_____

_____

If I had my life to live over again, I would_____

_____

_____

_____

My greatest happiness is_____

_____

_____

_____

_____

_____

_____

Other Thoughts

Here is a place to put the final touches on your book. If you ran out of room while writing on one of the pages, this is where you can continue your thoughts. If new ideas came to mind when you were going through the book but you couldn't find a heading that exactly suited your needs, here is a place where you can write about specific things that are important to you. In my book this is where I listed every single job I ever had. I also put some poetry here.

Including your own headings in this section, like those that were provided in the rest of the book, may help you to write about a topic that you want to record. You may also want to come back to your book at a later time and add more of your life stories. This is a place where you can insert those stories that combine to make the treasure that is you.

_____

_____

_____

_____

_____

_____

_____

_____

_____

_____

_____

_____

_____

_____

_____

_____

_____

_____

_____

_____